The SILE Book

The SILE Book

Simon Cozens

Table of Contents

Chapter 1
What is SILE?

SILE is a typesetting system. Its job is to produce beautiful printed documents. The best way to understand what SILE is and what it does is to compare it to other systems which you may have heard of.

1.1 SILE versus Word

When most people produce printed documents using a computer, they usually use software such as Word (part of Microsoft Office) or Writer (part of Open/LibreOffice) or similar–word processing software. SILE is not a word processor; it is a typesetting system. There are several important differences.

The job of a word processor is to produce a document that looks exactly like what you type on the screen. SILE takes what you type and considers it instructions for producing a document that looks as good as possible.

For instance, in a word processor, you keep typing and when you hit the right margin, your cursor will move to the next line. It is showing you where the lines will break. SILE doesn't show you where the lines will break, because it doesn't know yet. You can type and type and type as long a line as you like, and when SILE comes to process your instructions, it will consider your input (up to) three times over in order to work out how to best to break the lines to form a paragraph. Did we end two successive lines with a hyphenated word? Go back and try again.

Similarly for page breaks. When you type into a word processor, at some point you will spill over onto a new page. In SILE, you keep typing, because the page breaks are determined after considering the layout of the whole document.

Word processors often describe themselves as WYSIWYG–What You See Is What You Get. SILE is cheerfully *not* WYSIWYG. In fact, you don't see what you get until you get it. Rather, SILE documents are prepared initially in a *text editor*–a piece of software which focuses on the text itself and not what it looks like–and then ran through SILE in order to produce a PDF document.

In other words, SILE is a *language* for describing what you want to happen, and SILE will make certain formatting decisions about the best way for those instructions to be turned into print.

1.2 SILE versus TeX

Ah, some people will say, that sounds very much like TeX.[1] If you don't know much about TeX or don't care, you can probably skip this section.

But it's true. SILE owes an awful lot of its heritage to TeX. It would be terribly immodest to claim that a little project like SILE was a worthy successor to the ancient and venerable creation of the Professor of the Art of Computer Programming, but... really, SILE is basically a modern rewrite of TeX.

TeX was one of the earliest typesetting systems, and had to make a lot of design decisions somewhat in a vacuum. Some of those design decisions have stood the test of time–and TeX is still an extremely well-used typesetting system more than thirty years after its inception, which is a testament to its design and performance–but many others have not. In fact, most of the development of TeX since Knuth's era has involved removing his early decisions and replacing them with technologies which have become the industry standard: we use TrueType fonts, not METAFONTs (xetex); PDFs, not DVIs (pstex, pdftex); Unicode, not 7-bit ASCII (xetex again); markup languages and embedded programming languages, not macro languages (xmltex, luatex). At this point, the parts of TeX that people actually *use* are 1) the box-and-glue model, 2) the hyphenation algorithm, and 3) the line-breaking algorithm.

SILE follows TeX in each of these three areas; it contains a slavish port of the TeX line-breaking algorithm which has been tested to produce exactly the same output as TeX given equivalent input. But as SILE is itself written in an interpreted language,[2] it is very easy to extend or alter the behaviour of the SILE typesetter.

For instance, one of the things that TeX can't do particularly well is typesetting on a grid. This is something that people typesetting bibles really need to

---

1. Except that, being TeX users, they will say "Ah, that sounds very much like TeX".
2. And if the phrase TeX capacity exceeded is familiar to you, you should already be getting excited.

have. There are various hacks to try to make it happen, but they're all horrible. In SILE, you can alter the behaviour of the typesetter and write a very short add-on package to enable grid typesetting.

Of course, nobody uses plain TeX–they all use LaTeX equivalents plus a huge repository of packages available from the CTAN. SILE does not benefit from the large ecosystem and community that has grown up around TeX; in that sense, TeX will remain streets ahead of SILE for some time to come. But in terms of *capabilities*, SILE is already certainly equivalent to, if not somewhat more advanced than, TeX.

1.3 SILE versus InDesign

The other tool that people reach for when designing printed material on a computer is InDesign.

InDesign is a complex, expensive, commercial publishing tool. It's highly graphical–you click and drag to move areas of text and images around the screen. SILE is a free, open source typesetting tool which is entirely text-based; you enter commands in a separate editing tool, save those commands into a file, and hand it to SILE for typesetting. And yet the two systems do have a number of common features.

In InDesign, text is flowed into *frames* on the page. On the left, you can see an example of what a fairly typical InDesign layout might look like.

SILE also uses the concept of frames to determine where text should appear on the page, and so it's possible to use SILE to generate page layouts which are more flexible and more complex than that afforded by TeX.

Another thing which people use InDesign for is to turn structured data in XML format–catalogues, directories and the like–into print. The way you do this in InDesign is to declare what styling should apply to each XML element, and as the data is read in, InDesign formats the content according to the rules that you have declared.

You can do exactly the same thing in SILE, except you have a lot more control over how the XML elements get styled, because you can run any SILE command you like for a given element, including calling out to Lua code to style a piece of XML. Since SILE is a command-line filter, armed with appropriate styling instructions you can go from an XML file to a PDF in one shot. Which is quite nice.

In the final chapters of this book, we'll look at some extended examples of creating a *class file* for styling a complex XML document into a PDF with SILE.

1.4 Conclusion

SILE takes some textual instructions and turns them into PDF output. It has features inspired by TeX and InDesign, but seeks to be more flexible, extensible and programmable than them. It's useful both for typesetting documents such as this one written in the SILE language, and as a processing system for styling and outputting structured data.

Chapter 2
Getting Started

Now that we understand some of what SILE is about and what it seeks to do, let's dive into SILE itself.

2.1 A Basic SILE Document

Before we even show you how to use SILE, let's have a look at an example of what SILE documents look like. This is the input that we're going to feed to SILE, which it is going to process and turn into a PDF file.

These documents are plain text files; when you create your own SILE files, you will need to create them in a plain text editor such as vi or emacs on Unix, Sublime Text, TextMate or TextEdit on OS X, or Notepad or Notepad+ on Windows, save them as a text file and then use them as input to SILE. Trying to create these files in a word processor such as Word will not work, as they will not be saved with the word processor's formatting, rather than in a plain text format.

To begin with, here's the most basic SILE file of all:

```
\begin[papersize=a4]{document}
Hello SILE!
\end{document}
```

We'll pick apart this document in the next chapter, but for now take it on trust that this is what a SILE document looks like.

At risk of belabouring the obvious, this is going to produce an A4-sized PDF document, with the text Hello SILE at the top left, and the page number (1) centered at the bottom. How are we going to get to that PDF?

2.2 Installing

First of all, we need to get hold of SILE and get it running on our computer. Downloads of SILE can be obtained from the home page at `http://www.sile-typesetter.org/`.

SILE requires a number of other software packages to be installed on the computer before it can work—Cairo, Pango and Lua. On OS X machines running Homebrew (always a good idea for OS X machines), you will need to run

- `brew install cairo pango lua luarocks`

On DEB-based Linux machines such as Debian and Ubuntu, try

- `apt-get install libcairo-gobject2 libpango1.0-0 lua5.1 luarocks`

Once these dependencies are installed, you also need to install some Lua libraries:

- `luarocks install stdlib lgi lpeg luaexpat inspect luaepnf luarepl cassowary`

Now we should be finally really to go. Unpack the file that you downloaded from SILE's home page, and change to that directory. You can now run SILE as is, uninstalled:

- `./sile examples/simple.sil`

If all has gone well, this should produce a file `examples/simple.pdf`.

Most users of SILE will want to install the `sile` command and SILE's library files onto their system; this can be done with

- `lua install.lua`

Now the `sile` command is available from any directory.

2.3 Running SILE

Let's move to a new directory, and in a text editor, create the file `hello.sil`. Copy in the content above and save the file. Now at your command line run:

- `sile hello`

(SILE will automatically provide the extension `.sil` to input files if it is not provided by the user.)

Once again, this should produce an output file `hello.pdf`. Congratulations–you have just typeset your first document with SILE.

2.4 Let's Do Something Cool

In examples/article-template.xml, you will find a typical DocBook 5.0 article. Normally turning DocBook to print involves a curious dance of XSLT processors, format object processors and/or strange LaTeX packages. But SILE can read XML files and it also comes with a docbook class, which tells SILE how to render (admittedly, a subset of) the DocBook tags onto a page.

Turning examples/article-template.xml into examples/article-template.pdf is now as simple as:

```
% ./sile -I docbook examples/article-template.xml
This is SILE 0.9.0
Loading docbook
<classes/docbook.sil><examples/article-template.xml>[1] [2] [3]
```

The -I flag loads up a *class* before reading the input file; after this has been loaded, the DocBook file can be read directly and its tags interpreted as SILE commands.

In Chapter 10, we'll look at how the docbook class works, and how you can define processing expectations for other XML formats.

Getting Started

Chapter 3
SILE's Input Language

Let's now go back and reconsider the first SILE file we saw:

```
\begin[papersize=a4]{document}
Hello SILE!
\end{document}
```

A document starts with a \begin{document} command, which *must* define the paper size, and ends with \end{document}. In between, SILE documents are made up of two elements: text to be typeset on the page, such as "Hello SILE!" in our example, and commands.

Paper sizes

SILE knows about the ISO standard A, B and C series paper sizes, as well as the following traditional sizes: letter, note, legal, executive, halfletter, halfexecutive, statement, folio, quarto, ledger, tabloid.

If you need a paper size for your document which is not one of the standards, then you can specify it by dimensions: papersize=<basic length> x <basic length>*.*

Dimensions

SILE knows a number of ways of specifying lengths. A <basic length> *as mentioned above can be specified as a floating-point number followed by a dimension abbreviation. Acceptable dimensions are printer's points* (pt)*, millimeters* (mm)*, centimeters* (cm) *or inches.* (in) *For instance a standard B-format book can be specified* papersize=198mm x 129mm*. Later we will meet some other ways of specifying lengths.*

3.1 Ordinary text

On the whole, ordinary text isn't particularly interesting–it's just typeset.

TeX users may have an expectation that SILE will do certain things with ordinary text as well. For instance, if you place two straight-backquotes into a TeX document (like this: ``) then TeX will magically turn that into a double opening quote ("). SILE won't do this. If you want a double opening quote, you have to ask for one. Similarly, en- and em-dashes have to be input as actual Unicode en- and em-dashes, rather than -- or --- respectively.

There are only a few bits of cleverness that happen around ordinary text.

The first is that space is not particularly significant. If you write `Hello SILE!` with three spaces, you get the same output as if you write `Hello SILE!` with just one.

Similarly, you can place a line break anywhere you like in the input file, and it won't affect the output because SILE considers each paragraph at a time and computes the appropriate line breaks for the paragraph based on the width of the line available. In other words, if your input file says

---

```
Lorem ipsum dolor sit amet, consectetur adipisicing elit, sed do eiusmod
tempor incididunt ut labore et dolore magna aliqua. Ut enim ad minim veniam,
quis nostrud exercitation ullamco laboris nisi ut aliquip ex ea commodo
consequat. Duis aute irure dolor in reprehenderit in voluptate velit esse
cillum dolore eu fugiat nulla pariatur. Excepteur sint occaecat cupidatat non
proident, sunt in culpa qui officia deserunt mollit anim id est laborum.
```

---

you might not necessarily get a line break after 'eiusmod'; you'll get a line break wherever is most appropriate. In the context of this document, you'll get:

Lorem ipsum dolor sit amet, consectetur adipisicing elit, sed do eiusmod tempor

---

incididunt ut labore et dolore magna aliqua. Ut enim ad minim veniam, quis nostrud exercitation ullamco laboris nisi ut aliquip ex ea commodo consequat. Duis aute irure dolor in reprehenderit in voluptate velit esse cillum dolore eu fugiat nulla pariatur. Excepteur sint occaecat cupidatat non proident, sunt in culpa qui officia deserunt mollit anim id est laborum.

When you want to end a paragraph, you need to input two line breaks in a row, like this:

```
Paragraph one.

Paragraph two.
This is not paragraph three.

This is paragraph three.
```

The second clever thing that happens around ordinary text is that a few--four, in fact–characters have a special meaning to SILE. All of these will be familiar to TeX users.

We've seen that a *backslash* is used to start a command, and we'll look into commands in more detail soon. *Left and right curly braces* ({, }) are used for grouping, particularly in command arguments. Finally, a *percent sign* is used as a comment character, meaning that everything from the percent to the end of the line is ignored by SILE. If you want to actually typeset these characters, prepend a backslash to them: \\ produces '\', \{ produces '{', \} produces '}', and \% produces '%'.

The third clever thing is SILE will automatically hyphenate text at the end of a line if it feels this will make the paragraph shape look better. Text is hyphenated according to the current language options in place. By default, text is assumed to be in English unless SILE is told otherwise. In the Latin text above, we turned hyphenation off.

The final clever thing is that, where fonts declare ligatures (where two or more letters are merged into one in order to make them visually more attractive), SILE automatically applies the ligature. So if you type affluent fishing then, (depending on your font), your output might look like: 'affluent fishing.' If you specifically want to break up the ligature, then insert an empty group (using the grouping characters { and }) in the middle of the ligature: af{}f{}luent f{}ishing: affluent fishing

3.2 Commands

Typically (and we'll unpack that statement later), SILE commands are made up of a backslash followed by a command name, and a document starts with a \begin{document} command and ends with \end{document}.

A command may also take two other optional components: some *parameters*, and an *argument*. The \begin command at the start of the document is an example of this.[1]

```
\begin[papersize=a4]{document}
```

The parameters to a command are enclosed in square brackets and take the form *key=value*; multiple parameters are separated by commas or semicolons, as in [key1=value1,k Spaces around the keys are not significant; we could equally write that as [key1 = value1; key2 = value2; ...]. The optional argument (of which there can only be at most one) is enclosed in curly braces.[2]

Here are a few more examples of SILE commands:

```
\eject
% A command with no parameters or argument

\font[family=Times,size=10pt]          % Parameters, but no argument
```

---

1. Strictly speaking \begin isn't actually a command but we'll pretend that it is for now and get to the details in a moment.
2. TeX users may forget this and try adding a command argument "bare", without the braces. This won't work; in SILE, the braces are mandatory.

```
\chapter{Introducing SILE}          % Argument but no parameters

\font[family=Times,size=10pt]{Hi there!}   % Parameters and argument
```

3.3 Environments

Commands like \chapter and \em (emphasises text by making it italic) are normally used to enclose a relatively small piece of text; a few lines at most. Where you want to enclose a larger piece of the document, you can use an *environment*; an environment begins with \begin{*name*} and encloses all the text up until the corresponding \end{*name*}. We've already seen an example, the document environment, which must enclose the *entire* document.

Here is a secret: there is absolutely no difference between a command and an environment. In other words, the following two forms are equivalent:

```
\font[family=Times,size=10pt]{Hi there!}

\begin[family=Times,size=10pt]{font}
Hi there!
\end{font}
```

However, in some cases the environment form of the command will be easier to read and will help you to be clearer on where the command begins and ends.

3.4 The XML Flavour

While we're on the subject of alternative forms, SILE can actually process its input in a completely different file format. What we've seen so far has been SILE's "TeX-like flavor", but if the first character of the input file is an angle bracket (<) then SILE will interpret its input as an XML file. (If it isn't well-formed XML, then SILE will get very upset.)

Any XML tags within the input file will then be regarded as SILE commands, and tag attributes are interpreted as command parameters; from then on, the two file formats are exactly equivalent, with one exception: instead of a <document> tag, SILE documents can be enclosed in *any* tag. (Although <sile> is conventional for SILE documents.)

In other words, the XML form of the above document would be:

```
<sile papersize="a4">
Hello SILE!
</sile>
```

Commands without an argument need to be well-formed self-closing XML tags (for instance, <break/>), and commands with parameters should have well-formed attributes. The example above, in XML flavor, would look like this:

```
<font family="Times" size="10pt">Hi there!</font>
```

We don't expect humans to write their documents in SILE's XML flavor—the TeX-like flavor is much better for that—but having an XML flavor allows for computers to deal with SILE a lot more easily. One could create graphical user interfaces to edit SILE documents, or convert other XML formats to SILE.

However, there is an even smarter way of processing XML with SILE. For this, you need to know that you can define your own SILE commands, which can range from very simple formatting to fundamentally changing the way that SILE operates. If you have a file in some particular XML format–let's say it's a DocBook file—and you define SILE commands for each possible DocBook tag, then the DocBook file becomes a valid SILE input file, as-is.

In the final two chapters, we'll provide some examples of defining SILE commands and processing XML documents.

Chapter 4
Some Useful SILE Commands

We're going to organise our tour of SILE by usage; we'll start by giving you the most useful commands that you'll need to get started typesetting documents using SILE, and then we'll gradually move into more and more obscure corners as the documentation progresses.

4.1 Fonts

The most basic command for altering the look of the text is the \font command; it takes two forms:

- \font[*parameters...*]{*argument*}
- \font[*parameters...*]

The first form sets the given argument text in the specified font; the second form changes the font used to typeset text from this point on.

So, for instance:

```
Small text
\font[size=15pt]Big text!
\font[size=30pt]{Bigger text}
Still big text!
```

---

produces

Small text

Big text!

Bigger text

Still big text!

As you can see, one possible attribute is size, which can be specified as a SILE <dimension>. A <dimension> is like a <basic length> (described above) but with a few extra possible dimensions which are relative to the size of the *current* font: ex units (ex), em units (em), and en units (en).

The full list of attributes to the \font command are:

• *size*: as above.

• *family*: the name of the font to be selected. SILE should know about all the fonts installed on your system, so that fonts can be specified by their name. In the XML flavor of SILE, you can specify the font family as a CSS-style 'stack' delimited by commas.

• *style*: can be normal or italic.

• *variant*: can be normal or smallcaps.

• *weight*: a CSS-style numeric weight ranging from 100, through 200, 300, 400, 500, **600**, **700**, **800** to **900**. Not all fonts will support all weights (many just have two), but SILE will choose the closest.

• *language*: The two letter (ISO639-1) language code for the text. This will affect both font shaping and hyphenation.

It's quite fiddly to be always changing font specifications manually; later we'll see some ways to automate the process. SILE provides the \em{...} command as a shortcut for \font[style=italic]{...}. There is no shortcut for boldface, because boldface isn't good typographic practice and so we don't want to make it easy for you to make bad books.

4.2 Document Structure

SILE provides a number of different *classes* of document (similar to La-TeX classes). By default, you get the *plain* class, which has very little support for structured documents. There is also the *book* class, which adds support for right and left page masters, running headers, footnotes, and chapter, section and subsection headings.

To use the commands in this section, you will need to request the *book* class by specifying in your \begin{document} command '[class=book]'; for example, the document you are currently reading begins with the command \begin[papersize=a4,class=book]{document}.

4.2.1 Chapters and Sections

You can divide your document into different sections using the commands \chapter{...}, \section{...} and \subsection{...}. The argument to each command is the name of the chapter or section respectively; chapters will be opened on a new right-hand page, and the chapter name will form the left running header. Additionally the section name and number will form the right running header.

Chapters, sections and subsections will be automatically numbered starting from 1; to alter the numbering, see the documentation for the counters *package in the next chapter.*

This subsection begins with the command \subsection{Chapters and Sections}.

4.2.2 Footnotes

Footnotes can be added to a book with the \footnote{...} command.[1] The argument to the command will be set as a footnote at the bottom of the page; footnotes are automatically numbered from 1 at the start of each chapter.

4.3 Indentation and Spacing

Paragraphs in SILE normally begin with an indentation (by default, 20

---

1. Like this: \footnote{Like this.}

points in width). To turn this off, you can use the \noindent command at the start of a paragraph. (This current paragraph doesn't need to call \noindent because \section and \chapter automatically call it for the text following the heading.) A \noindent can be cancelled by following it with an \indent.

To increase the vertical space between paragraphs or other elements, the commands \smallskip, \medskip and \bigskip are available to add a 3pt, 6pt and 12pt gap respectively. There will be a \bigskip after this paragraph.

There are also some commands to increase the horizontal space in a line; from the smallest to the largest, \thinspace (1/6th of an em), \enspace (1 en), \quad (1 em), and \qquad (2em).

You can center a paragraph of text
by wrapping it in the center environment. (\begin{center}
... \end{center}). This paragraph is centered on the page.

4.4 Breaks

SILE automatically determines line and page breaks; in later chapters we will introduce some *settings* which can be used to tweak this process. However, SILE's plain class also provides some commands to help the process on its way.

Between paragraphs, the \break command requests a *frame break* at the given location. (The commands \framebreak and \eject are also available as synonyms.) Where there are multiple frames on a page—for instance, in a document with multiple columns—the current frame will be ended and typesetting will recommence at the top of the next frame. \pagebreak (also known as \supereject) is a more forceful variant, and ensures that a new page is opened even if there are remaining frames on the page. A less forceful variant is \goodbreak, which suggests to SILE that this is a good point to break a page. The opposite is \nobreak which requests that, if at all possible, SILE does not break at the given point.

A neutral variant is \allowbreak, which allows SILE to break at a point that it would otherwise not consider as suitable for breaking.

Within a paragraph, these commands have a different meaning. The \break command requests a *line* break at the given location, and, *mutatis mutandis*, so do \goodbreak, \nobreak and \allowbreak. If you want to be absolutely sure that you are inhibiting a *page* break, you can say \novbreak.

SILE normally fully-justifies text–that is, it tries to alter the spacing between words so that the text stretches across the full width of the column. An alternative to full justification is ragged right margin formatting, where the spacing between words is constant but the right hand side of the paragraph may not line up. Ragged right is often used for children's books and for frames with narrow columns such as newspapers. To switch to ragged right formatting, use the command \raggedright. To switch back, use \justified. This paragraph is set ragged right.

4.5 Hyphenation and Language

SILE hyphenates words based on its current language. (Language is set using the \font command above.) At present the only hyphenation patterns available for SILE are for English and Greek, although it is not difficult for TeX users to produce additional pattern files. (Please send them to me if you do!)

SILE comes with a special "language" called xx, which has no hyphenation patterns available. If you switch to this language, text will not be hyphenated. The command \nohyphenation{...} is provided as a shortcut for \font[language=xx]{...}.

4.6 Including Other Files and Code

To make it easier for you to author a large document, you can break your SILE document up into multiple files. For instance, you may wish to put each chapter into a separate file; you may wish to develop a file of user-defined commands (see chapter 6) and keep this separate from the main body of the document. You will then need the ability to include one SILE file from another.

This ability is provided by the \include command. It takes one mandatory parameter, src=<*path*>, which represents the path to the file. So for instance, you may wish to write a thesis like this:

```
\begin[papersize=a4,class=thesis]{document}
\include[src=macros]
\include[src=chap1]
\include[src=chap2]
\include[src=chap3]
...
\include[src=endmatter]
\end{document}
```

\includes may be nested, in that file A can include file B which includes file C.

SILE is written in the Lua programming language, and the Lua interpreter is available at runtime. Just as one can run Javascript code from within a HTML document using a <script> tag, one can run Lua code from within a SILE document using a \script command. (It looks better in XML-flavor.) This command has two forms: \script[src=<*filename*>] which includes a Lua file, and \script{...} which runs Lua code inline.

Doing anything interesting inline requires knowledge of the internals of SILE, (thankfully the code is not that hard to read) but to get you started, the Lua function SILE.typesetter:typeset(...) will add text to a page, SILE.call("...") will call a SILE command, and SILE.typesetter:leaveHmode() ends the current paragraph and outputs the text. So, for example:

```
\begin{script}
  for i=1,10 do
    SILE.typesetter:typeset(i .. " x " .. i .. " = " .. i*i .. ". ")
    SILE.typesetter:leaveHmode()
    SILE.call("smallskip")
  end
\end{script}
```

produces the following output:

```
1 x 1 = 1.
2 x 2 = 4.
3 x 3 = 9.
4 x 4 = 16.
5 x 5 = 25.
6 x 6 = 36.
7 x 7 = 49.
8 x 8 = 64.
9 x 9 = 81.
10 x 10 = 100.
```

Some Useful SILE Commands

Chapter 5
SILE Packages

SILE comes with a number of packages which provide additional functionality. In fact, the actual "core" of SILE's functionality is very small and very extensible, with most of the interesting features being provided by add-on packages. SILE packages are written in the Lua programming language, and can define new commands, change the way that the SILE system operates, or indeed do anything that it's possible to do in Lua.

As mentioned above, loading a package is done through the \script command, which runs Lua code. By convention packages live in the packages/ subdirectory of either your working directory or SILE's installation directory. For instance, we'll soon be talking about the grid package, which normally can be found as /usr/local/lib/sile/packages/grid.lua. To load this, we'd say:

```
\script[src=packages/grid]
```

How SILE locates files

SILE searches for paths in a variety of directories: first, in the current directory; next, if the environment variable SILE_PATH is set, it will look in that directory; then it will look in the standard installation directories /usr/lib/sile and /usr/local/lib/sile. Unlike TeX, it does not descend into subdirectories when looking for a file, and so if you have arranged your personal macro, class or package files into subdirectories, you will need to provide a full relative path to them.

5.1 image

As well as processing text, SILE can also include images.

> *Image support is rather rudimentary at present due to limitations of the libraries that SILE uses.*

Loading the image package gives you the \img command, fashioned after the HTML equivalent. \img takes the following parameters: src=… must be the path to an image file *in PNG format*; you may also give height=… and/or width=… parameters to specify the output size of the image on the paper. If the size parameters are not given, then the image will be output at its 'natural' pixel size.

Here is a 200x243 pixel image output with \img[src=documentation/ gutenberg.png]:

Here it is with (respectively) \img[src=documentation/gutenberg.png, width=120px],
\img[src=documentation/gutenberg.png,height=200px], and
\img[src=documentation/gutenberg.png,width=120px,height=200px]:

Notice that images are typeset on the baseline of a line of text, rather like a very big letter.

5.2 rules

The rules package draws lines. It provides two commands.

The first command is \hrule, which draws a line of a given length and thickness, although it calls these width and height. (A box is just a square line.)

Lines are treated just like other text to be output, and so can appear in the middle of a paragraph, like this: ___ (that one was generated with \hrule[width=20pt, height=0.5pt].)

Like images, rules are placed along the baseline of a line of text.

The second command provided by rules is \underline, which underlines its contents.

Underlining is horrible typographic practice, and you should never do it.

(That was produced with \underline{never}.)

5.3 color

The color package allows you to temporarily change the color of the (virtual) ink that SILE uses to output text and rules. The package provides a \color command which takes one parameter, color=*<color specification>*, and typesets its argument in that color. The color specification is the same as HTML: it can be a RGB color value in #xxx or #xxxxxx format, where x represents a hexadecimal digit (#000 is black, #fff is white, #f00 is red and so on), or it can be one of the HTML and CSS named colors.

The   HTML   and   CSS   named   colors   can   be   found   at
`http://dev.w3.org/csswg/css-color/#named-colors`.

So, for example, this text is typeset with `\color[color=red]{…}`.

Here   is   a   rule   typeset   with   `\color[color=#22dd33]`:

5.4 grid

In normal typesetting, SILE determines the spacing between lines of type according to the following two rules:

• SILE tries to insert space between two successive lines so that their baselines are separated by a fixed distance called the `baselineskip`.

• If this first rule would mean that the bottom and the top of the lines are less than two points apart, then they are forced to be two points apart. (This distance is configurable, and called the `lineskip`)

The second rule is designed to avoid the situation where the first line has a long descender (letters such as g, q, j, p, etc.) which abuts a high ascender on the second line. (k, l, capitals, etc.)

In addition, the `baselineskip` contains a certain amount of 'stretch', so that the lines can expand if this would help with producing a page break at an optimal location, and similarly spacing between paragraphs can stretch or shrink.

The combination of all of these rules means that a line may begin at practically any point on the page.

An alternative way of typesetting is to require that lines begin at fixed points on a regular grid. Some people prefer the 'color' of pages produced by grid typesetting, and the method is often used when type-setting on very thin paper as lining up the lines of type on both sides of a page ensures that ink does not bleed through from the back to the front. Compare the following examples: on the left, the lines are guaranteed to fall in the same places on the recto (front) and the verso (back) of the paper; on the right, no such guarantee is made.

lorem   lorem

ipsum   ipsum

dolor   dolor

sit amet   sit amet

The grid package alters the way that the SILE's typesetter oper-ates so that the two rules above do not apply; lines are always aligned on a fixed grid, and spaces between paragraphs etc. are adjusted to conform to the grid. Loading the package adds two new commands to SILE: \grid[spacing=<dimension>] and \no-grid. The first turns on grid typesetting for the remainder of the document; the second turns it off again.

At the start of this section, we issued the command \grid[spacing= 15pt] to set up a regular 15-point grid. Here is some text typeset with the grid set up:

Lorem ipsum dolor sit amet, consectetur adipisicing elit, sed do eiusmod tempor incididunt ut labore et dolore magna aliqua. Ut enim ad minim veniam, quis nostrud exercitation ullamco laboris nisi ut aliquip ex ea commodo consequat. Duis aute irure dolor in reprehenderit in voluptate velit esse cillum dolore eu fugiat nulla pariatur. Excepteur sint occaecat cupidatat non proident, sunt in culpa qui officia deserunt mollit anim id est laborum.

And here is the same text after we issue \no-grid:

Lorem ipsum dolor sit amet, consectetur adipisicing elit, sed do eiusmod tempor incididunt ut labore et dolore magna aliqua. Ut enim ad minim veniam, quis nostrud exercitation ullamco laboris nisi ut aliquip ex ea commodo consequat. Duis aute irure dolor in reprehenderit in voluptate velit esse cillum dolore eu fugiat nulla pariatur. Excepteur sint occaecat cupidatat non proident, sunt in culpa qui officia deserunt mollit anim id est laborum.

5.5 verbatim

The verbatim package is useful when quoting pieces of computer code and other text for which formatting is significant. It changes SILE's settings so that text is set ragged right, with no hyphenation, no indentation and regular spacing. It tells SILE to honor multiple spaces, and sets a monospaced font.

Despite the name, verbatim *does not alter the way that SILE sees special characters. You still need to escape backslashes and braces: to produce a backslash, you need to write* \\.

Here is some text set in the verbatim environment:

```
function SILE.repl()
  if not SILE._repl then SILE.initRepl() end
  SILE._repl:run()
end
```

5.6 Packages usually used by other packages

In addition, there are certain packages that you *probably* don't need to use directly, as their main job is to provide more basic functionality to other packages and classes. Classes such as the book class compose functionality from different auxiliary packages.

5.6.1 footnotes

For instance, we've seen that the book class allows you to add footnotes to text with the \footnote command. This command is actually provided by the footnotes package. The book class loads up the package and tells it where to put the footnotes that are typeset, and the footnotes package takes care of formatting the footnotes. It does this by using a number of other packages that we will describe below.

5.6.2 counters

Various parts of SILE such as the footnotes package and the sectioning commands keep a counter of things going on: the current footnote number, the chapter number, and so on. The counters package allows you to set up, increment and typeset named counters. It provides the following commands:

• \set-counter[id=*<counter-name>*,value=*<value>*] – sets the counter called <counter-name> to the value given.

• \increment-counter[id=*<counter-name>*] – does the same as \set-counter except that when no value parameter is given, the counter is incremented by one.

• \show-counter[id=*<counter-name>*] – this typesets the value of the counter according to the counter's declared display type.

31

All of the commands in the counters package take an optional display=<*display-type*> parameter to set the display type of the counter.

The available display types are: arabic, the default; roman, for lower-case Roman numerals; and Roman for upper-case Roman numerals.

So, for example, the following SILE code:

```
\set-counter[id=mycounter, value=2]
\show-counter[id=mycounter]

\increment-counter[id=mycounter]
\show-counter[id=mycounter, display=roman]
```

---

produces:

2
iii

5.6.3 raiselower

If you don't want your images, rules or text to be placed along the baseline, you can use the raiselower package to move them up and down. (The footnote package uses this to superscript the footnote reference numbers.)

It provides two simple commands, \raise and \lower which both take a height=<*dimension*> parameter. They will respectively raise or lower their argument by the given height. The raised or lowered content will not alter the height or depth of the line.

Here is some text raised by three points; here is some text lowered by four points·

The previous paragraph was generated by:

```
Here is some text raised by \raise[height=3pt]{three points}; here is
```

```
some text lowered by \lower[height=4pt]{four points}.
```

5.6.4 frametricks

As we mentioned in the first chapter, SILE uses frames as an indication of where to put text onto the page. The frametricks package assists package authors by providing a number of commands to manipulate frames.

The most immediately useful is \showframe. This asks the output engine to draw a box and label around a particular frame. It takes an optional parameter id=<frame id>; if this is not supplied, the current frame is used. If the ID is all, then all frames declared by the current class are displayed.

The command \breakframevertical breaks the current frame in two at the specified location into an upper and lower frame. If the frame initially had the ID main, then main becomes the upper frame (before the command) and the lower frame (after the command) is called main_. We just issued a \breakframehorizontal command at the start of this paragraph, and now we will issue the command \showframe. As you can see, the current frame is called l_ and now begins at the start of the paragraph.

Similarly, the \breakframehorizontal command breaks the frame in two into a left and a right frame. The command takes an optional argument offset=<dimension>, specifying where on the line the frame should be split. If it is not supplied, the frame is split at the current position in the line.

The command \shiftframeedge allows you to reposition the current frame left or right. It takes left= and/or right= parameters, which can be positive or negative dimensions. It should only be used at the top of a frame, as it reinitializes the typesetter object.

Combining all of these commands, the \float command breaks the current frame, creates a small frame to hold a floating object (like the dropcap at the start of this sentence), flows text into the surrounding frame, and then, once text has descended past the floating object, moves the frame back into place again. It takes two optional pa-

33

rameters, bottomboundary=*<dimension>* and/or rightboundary= *<dimension>*, which open up additional space around the frame. At the start of this paragraph, I issued the command \float[bottomboundary=5pt] {\font[size=60pt]{C}}.

5.6.5 insertions

The footnotes package works by taking auxiliary material (the footnote content), shrinking the current frame and inserting it into the footnote frame. This is powered by the insertions package; it doesn't provide any user-visible SILE commands, but provides Lua functionality to other packages. TeX wizards may be interested to realise that insertions are implemented by an external add-on package, rather than being part of the SILE core.

5.6.6 twoside

The book class described in chapter 4 sets up left and right mirrored page masters; the twoside package is responsible for swapping between the two left and right frames, running headers and so on. It has no user-serviceable parts.

5.6.7 infonode

This package is only for class designers.

While typesetting a document, SILE first breaks a paragraph into lines, then arranges lines into a page, and later outputs the page. In other words, while it is looking at the text of a paragraph, it is not clear what page the text will eventually end up on. This makes it difficult to produce indexes, tables of contents and so on where one needs to know the page number for a particular element.

To get around this problem, the infonode allows you to insert *information nodes* into the text stream; when a page is outputted, these nodes are collected into a list, and a class's output routine can examine this list to determine which nodes fell on a particular page. infonode provides the \info command to put an information node into the text stream;

it has two required parameters, category= and value=. Categories are used to group similar sets of node together.

As an example, when typesetting a Bible, you may wish to display which range of verses are on each page as a running header. During the command which starts a new verse, you would insert an information node with the verse reference:

```
SILE.Commands["info"]( category = "references", value = ref , )
```

During the endPage method which is called at the end of every page, we look at the list of "references" information nodes:

```
local refs = SILE.scratch.info.thispage.references
local
runningHead = SILE.shaper.shape(refs[1] .. " - " .. refs[#refs])
SILE.typesetNaturally(rhFrame, runningHead);
```

Chapter 6
SILE Macros and Commands

One of the reasons that we use computers is that they are very good at doing repetitive jobs for us, so that we don't have to. Perhaps the most important skill in operating computers, and particularly in programming computers, is noticing areas where an action is being repeated, and allowing the computer to do the work instead of the human. In other words, Don't Repeat Yourself.

The same is true in operating SILE. After you have been using the system for a while, you will discover that there are patterns of input that you need to keep entering again and again.

6.1 A simple macro

For instance, let's suppose that we want to design a nice little "bumpy road" logo for SILE. (Afficionados of TeX and friends will be familar with the concept of bumpy road logos.) Our logo will look like this: SILE. It's not a great logo, but we'll use it as SILE's logo for the purposes of this section.

To typeset this logo, we need to ask SILE to: typeset an 'S'; typeset an 'I' lowered by a certain amount (half an ex, as it happens); typeset an 'L'; walk backwards along the line a tiny bit; typeset a smaller-sized 'E' raised by a certain amount.

In SILE code, that looks like:

```
S\lower[height=0.5ex]{I}L\glue[width=-
.2em]\raise[height=0.6ex]{\font[size=0.8em]{E}}
```

(Don't worry about the \glue command for the moment; we'll come back to that later.)

We've used our logo four times already in this chapter, and we don't want to have to input that whole monostrosity each time we do so. What we would like to do is tell the computer "this is S_I^L_E's logo; each time I enter \SILE, I want you to interpret that as S\lower[height=0.5ex]{I}L \glue[width=-.2em]\raise[height=0.6ex]{\font[size=0.8em]{E}}".

In other words, we want to define our own commands.

SILE[1] allows you to define your own commands in two ways. The simplest commands of all are those like \SILE above: "when I write \x, I want SILE to pretend that I had written X \Y Z instead." These are called *macros*, and the process of pretending is called *macro expansion*.

You can define these kinds of macros within a SILE file itself. In this very file, we entered:

```
\define[command=SILE]{
S\lower[height=0.5ex]{I}L\glue[width=-
.2em]\raise[height=0.6ex]{\font[size=0.8em]{E}}
}
```

We're using the built-in SILE command \define. \define takes an option called command; its value is the name of the command we are defining. The content of the \define command is a series of SILE instructions to be executed when the command is used.

At this point it's worth knowing the precise rules for allowable names of SILE commands.

Commands in XML-flavor input files must be allowable XML tag names or else your input files will not be well formed. Command names in TeX-flavor input files may consist of any number of alphanumeric characters, hyphens or colons. Additionally, any single character is a valid TeX-flavor command name. (Hence

---

1. Let's give up on the logo at this point.

\\ for typesetting a backslash.)

When it comes to defining commands, commands defined by an XML-flavor file can actually have any name that you like–even if they are not accessible from XML-favour! (You may define oddly-named commands in a XML-flavor SILE file and then use them in a TeX-flavor SILE file.) Commands defined in TeX-flavor obviously have to have names which are valid parameter values, or else they will not parse correctly either; parameter values happen to consist of any text up until the nearest comma, semicolon or closing square bracket.

6.2 Macro with content

Now let's move on to the next level; sometimes you will want to create commands which are not simply replacements, but which have arguments of their own. As an example, let's say we use the color package to turn a bit of text red like this. The usual way to do that is to say

```
\color[color=red]{like this}
```

However, we're not always going to want to be highlighting the words 'like this'. We might want to be able to highlight other text instead. We need the ability to wrap the command \color[color=red]{ ... } around our chosen content. In other words, we want to be able to define our own commands which take arguments.

The way we express this in SILE is with the \process command. \process is only valid within the context of a \define command (you'll mess everything up if you try using it somewhere else), and it basically means 'do whatever you were planning to do with the arguments to this command.' So if we want to a command which makes things red, we can say:

```
\define[command=red]{\color[color=red]{\process}}
...

Making things red is a \red{silly} way to emphasise text.
```

> *You can't call* \process *more than once within the same macro.*
>
> *In the definition of the* \chapter *command, we want to 1) display the chapter name in a big bold font, and 2) use the chapter name as the left running header. If you try writing the* \chapter *command as a macro, you will get stuck—once you've* \processed *the chapter name to display it in bold, you won't be able to process it again to set the running header.*
>
> *So the* \chapter *command cannot be written as a simple macro. The other way to implement your own commands is to write them in the Lua programming language, which is what happens for* \chapter. *We will see how to do this in later chapters.*
>
> *The* \define *command really is meant to be used just for simple things.*

6.3 Nesting macros

That said, one thing you can do is to call a macro within a macro. This should be obvious, because a macro is just a replacement for the current processing step—when SILE reads a macro command, it behaves as if you had entered the definition of the macro instead, and of course such a definition can contain other commands.

So it is possible even within the simple scope of macro processing to achieve quite a lot of automation.

For instance, within this book, there have been a number of notes—italicized paragraphs between two heavy lines with a left margin. These have been typeset with the \note command; this is not a built-in command but a macro specified within the documentation/macros.sil file included by this document. Here is one way to define \note, in XML flavour:

```
<define command="line">
  <par/><smallskip/><noindent/>
  <hrule width="450pt" height="0.3pt"/><par/>
  <novbreak/><smallskip/><novbreak/>
</define>
<define command="narrower">
  <set parameter="document.lskip" value="24pt"/>
  <process>
  <set parameter="document.lskip" value="0pt"/>
</end>
<define command="notefont"><font
style="italic" size="10pt"><process/></font></notefont>
<define command="note">
  <narrower>
    <line/>
    <notefont><process/></notefont>
    <line/>
  </narrower>
</define>
```

The only command we have not yet met here is \set, which we will now investigate.

Chapter 7
SILE Settings

As well as commands, SILE offers a variety of knobs and levers which affect how it does its job. Changing these parameters can have anything from a subtle to a dramatic effect on the eventual document. External packages may declare their own settings (although none of the packages which ship with SILE happen to do so), but here we will run through the settings which are built into the SILE system itself.

Settings in SILE are *namespaced* so that 1) the name of the setting gives you some kind of clue as to what area of the system it will affect, and 2) packages can define their own settings without worrying that they will be interfering with other packages or the SILE internals. Namespacing of settings takes the form *area.name*–so for instance, typesetter.orphanpenalty is the setting which changes how the typesetter penalizes orphan (end-of-paragraph) lines.

The interface to changing settings from within a SILE document is the \set commmand. It take two options: a *parameter* option which expresses which setting is being changed, and a *value* option which expresses the value to which the setting is being changed. As an example:

```
\set[parameter=typesetter.orphanpenalty, value=250]
```

Now, let's begin looking at what each of the built-in settings does, starting from the most obvious and moving towards the most subtle.

7.1 Spacing Settings

In our \note example, we saw the setting document.lskip. This is a *glue* parameter which is added to the left side of every line. Setting this to a positive length effectively increases the left margin of the text. Similarly, document.rskip adds some space to the right side of every line.

Glue

A glue parameter is slightly different from an ordinary dimensioned length. Glue basically means 'space,' but as well as signifying a length, it also has two additional optional components: stretch and skip, specified as <dimension> plus <dimension> minus <dimension>. *The first dimension is the basic length; the stretch is the maximum length that can be added to it, and the shrink is some length that can be taken away from it. For instance,* 12pt plus 3pt minus 6pt *specifies a space that would ideally by 12 points, but can expand or contract from a minimum of 9 points to a maximum of 18 points.*

So, for instance, to center a paragraph, you can set the margin parameters like so:

```
\set[parameter=document.lskip,value=20pt
plus 1000pt]% or similar ridiculous quantity
\set[parameter=document.rskip,value=20pt plus 1000pt]
```

This will narrow the left and right margins of the paragraph by at least 20 points, but adds a large stretch which will be evenly distributed on both the left and right side of each line, leaving the text of the paragraph sitting in the middle.

The indentation at the start of each paragraph is controlled by the setting document.parindent; this is a glue parameter, and by default it's set to 20pt with no stretch and shrink. Actually, the amount added to the start of the paragraph is current.parindent. After each paragraph, current.parident is reset to the value of document.parindent. The \noindent command works by setting current.parindent to zero.

How would you make a paragraph like this with a 'hanging' indentation? We've set the document.lskip to 20 points, and the current.parindent to *minus* 20 points. (In other words, we called: \set[parameter=document.lskip,value=20pt] and \set[parameter=current.parindent, value=-20pt].)

The space between *paragraphs* is set with the glue parameter document.parskip. It's normally set to five points with one point of stretchability.

As we mentioned in the section on grid typesetting, the rules for spacing between *lines* within a paragraph is determined by two rules. Let's reiterate those rules now in terms of settings:

• SILE tries to insert space between two successive lines to make their baselines exactly document.baselineskip apart.

• If this first rule would mean that the bottom and the top of the lines are less than document.lineskip apart, then they are forced to be document.lineskip apart.

The final spacing setting is document.spaceskip. Normally the size of the space between *words* is determined by the width of the space character in the current font. If you want to set it explicitly, you can set the document.spaceskip setting. If you want to go back to the default (measuring the space character of the font), then you need to *unset* the setting. To unset it, just call \set with no *value* parameter: \set[parameter=document.spaceskip].

7.2 Typesetter settings

The settings which affect SILE's spacing controls have the most obvious effect on a document; the typesetter itself has some knobs that can be twiddled:

typesetter.widowpenalty and typesetter.orphanpenalty[1] affect how strongly SILE is averse to leaving stray lines at the start and end of pages. A *widow* happens when a page is broken leaving one line at the bottom of a page; an *orphan* line is the last line in a paragraph broken off at the top of the page. By default, the *penalty* attached to breaking the page at one of these places is 150 penalty points. This value can be any number up to 10000, which means "never break at this point."

SILE automatically inserts a piece of massively stretchable glue at the end of each paragraph; without this, the justification algorithm would apply justification to the entire paragraph, including the last fine, and produce a fully justified paragraph. (Normally we want the last line of a justified paragraph to be left-aligned.) The size of this glue is defined in the setting typesetter.parfillskip. Its default value is 0pt plus 10000pt but for this current paragraph, we have unset it.

Finally, the typesetter needs to know what separates a paragraph. Normally, this is two consecutive newlines in the input. However, when

---

1. TeX users, please notice the renaming.

you are dealing with transforming XML input, this may not be a good assumption; in that case, you can set the setting typesetter.parseppattern to a Lua pattern. Its default setting is \n\n+. Additionally, the way that multiple spaces in an input are collapsed into one space is by means of the shaper.spacepattern setting. By default, this is set to %s+ (any number of spaces are interpreted as one space.) If you want to preserve spacing, so that two spaces in the input are typeset as two spaces in the output, you can set the space pattern to %s.

7.3 Linebreaking settings

SILE's linebreaking algorithm is lifted entirely from TeX, and so maintains the same level of customizability as TeX. Here is a quick run-down of the settings applicable to the line-breaking algorithm. You are expected to know what you are doing with these.

• linebreak.tolerance: How bad a breakpoint is before it is rejected by the algorithm. (Default: 500)

• linebreak.pretolerance: If there are no breakpoints better than this, the paragraph is considered for hyphenation. (Default: 100)

• linebreak.adjdemerits: Additional demerits which are accumulated in the course of paragraph building when two consecutive lines are visually incompatible. In these cases, one line is built with much space for justification, and the other one with little space. (Default: 10000)

• linebreak.looseness: How many lines the current paragraph should be made longer than normal. (Default: 0)

• linebreak.prevGraf: The number of lines in the paragraph last added to the vertical list.

• linebreak.emergencyStretch: Assumed extra stretchability in lines of a paragraph. (Default: 0)

• linebreak.linePenalty: Penalty value associated with each line break. (Default: 10)

• linebreak.hyphenPenalty: Penalty associated with break at a hyphen.

(Default: 50)

• linebreak.doubleHyphenDemerits: Penalty for consecutive lines ending with a hyphen. (Default: 10000)

7.4 Settings from Lua

Most of the time you will not be fiddling with these settings at the SILE layer, because complex layout commands are expected to be implemented in Lua. The following SILE functions access the settings system from inside Lua:

• SILE.settings.set(*<parameter>*, *value*): sets a setting.

> You should note that, while in the SILE layer, the \set command does its best to turn the textual description of a type into the appropriate Lua type for the value. SILE.settings.set *does not do that; it expects the value to be of the appropriate type: lengths need to be a* SILE.Length *object, glue must be* Glue *and so on.*

• SILE.settings.get(*<parameter>*): retrieves the current setting of the parameter.

• SILE.settings.temporarily(*function*): Saves all settings, runs the function and then restores all settings afterwards.

• SILE.settings.declare(*<specification>*): Declares a new setting. See the base settings in settings.lua for examples of how to call this. A class or package should namespace its settings with <package>.<setting>.

Chapter 8
The Nitty Gritty

We are finally at the bottom of our delve into SILE's commands and settings. Here are the basic building blocks out of which all of the other operations in SILE are created; in fact, they are the basic building blocks of SILE's operation.

At this point, it is expected that you are a class designer, and will be able to follow the details of how SILE implements these commands and features; we will also explain how to interact with these components at the Lua level.

8.1 Boxes, Glue and Penalties

SILE's job is, looking at it in very abstract terms, all about arranging little boxes on a page. Some of those boxes have letters in them, and are those letters are such-and-such a number of points wide and such-and-such a number of points high; some of the boxes are empty but are there just to take up space; when a horizontal row of boxes has been decided (i.e. when a line break is determined) then the whole row of boxes is put into another box and the vertical list of boxes are then arranged to form a page.

Conceptually, then, SILE knows about a few different basic components: horizontal boxes (such as a letter); horizontal glue (the stretchable, shrinkable space between words); vertical boxes (a line of text); vertical glue (the space between lines and paragraphs); and penalties (information about when and when not to break lines and pages).[1]

The most immediately useful of these are horizontal and vertical glue. It is possible to explicitly add horizontal and vertical glue into

---

1. Additionally there are two more types of box that SILE cares about: N-nodes and discretionaries.

SILE's processing stream using the \glue and \skip commands. These take a width and a height parameter respectively, both of which are glue dimensions. So, for instance, the \smallskip command is the equivalent of \skip[height=3pt plus 1pt minus 1pt]; \thinspace is defined as being \glue[width=0.16667em].

Similarly, there is a \penalty command for inserting penalty nodes; \break is defined as \penalty[penalty=-10000] and \nobreak is \penalty[penalty=10000].

You can also create horizontal and vertical boxes from within SILE. One obvious reason for doing so would be to explicitly avoid material being broken up by a page or line break; another reason for doing so would be that once you box some material up, you then know how wide or tall it is. The \hbox and \vbox commands put their contents into a box; when called from Lua, they also *return* the new box.

8.1.1 From Lua

SILE's Lua interface contains a nodefactory for creating boxes and glue. Before we get into that, however, you need to know that glue measurements in SILE should always be specified in terms of SILE.length objects; these are "three-dimensional" lengths, in that they consist of a base length plus stretch and shrink. To construct a SILE.length:

```
local l = SILE.length.new({ length = x, stretch = y, shrink = z})
```

Now we can construct horizontal and vertical glue:

```
local glue  = SILE.nodefactory.newGlue ({ width  =  l})
local vglue = SILE.nodefactory.newVglue({ height =  l})
```

SILE's typesetting is organised by the SILE.typesetter object; it maintains two queues of material that it is working on–the node queues (SILE.typesetter.state.nodes) contains new horizontal boxes and glue that are going to be broken up into lines soon; and the output queue (SILE.typesetter.state.outputQueue) which consists of vertical material (lines) which are going to be broken up into pages. Line breaking and page breaking happens when the typesetter moves between horizontal and vertical mode; you can force this to happen by calling the function SILE.typesetter:leaveHmode(). The SILE-level command for forcing a paragraph end is \par.

So, if you want to manually add a vertical space to the output, first ensure that material in the current paragraph has been all properly boxed-up and moved onto the output queue by calling SILE.typesetter: leaveHmode(); then add your desired glue to the output queue.

Adding boxes and glue to the typesetter's queues is such a common operation that the typesetter has some utility methods to construct the nodes and add them for you:

```
SILE.typesetter:leaveHmode()
SILE.typesetter:pushVglue({ height = 1 })
```

Adding boxes yourself is a little more complicated, because boxes need to know how to display themselves on the page. To facilitate this, they normally store a value and an outputYourself member function. For instance, the image package actually does something very simple; it adds a horizontal box to the node queue which knows the width and height of the image, the source, and instructions to the output engine to display the image:

```
SILE.typesetter:pushHbox({
  width= …,
  height= …,
```

```
    depth= 0,
    value= options.src,
    outputYourself= function (this, typesetter, line)
      SILE.outputter.drawPNG(this.value,
        typesetter.frame.state.cursorX,
typesetter.frame.state.cursorY-this.height,
        this.width,this.height
      );
    typesetter.frame:moveX(this.width)
end});
```

Adding horizontal and vertical penalties to the typesetter's queues is similarly done with the SILE.typesetter:pushPenalty({penalty = x}) and SILE.typesetter:pushVpenalty({penalty = y}) methods.

8.2 Frames

As we have previously mentioned, SILE arranges text into frames on the page. Normally those frames are defined by your document class, but you can actually create your own frames on a per-page basis using the \pagetemplate and \frame commands. There are very few situations in which you will actually want to do this, but if you can understand this, it will help you to understand how to define your own document classes.

For instance, in a couple of pages time we're going to implement a two-column layout. SILE uses a *constraint solver* system to declare its frames, which means that you can tell it how the frames relate to each other and it will compute where the frames should be physically placed on the page.

Here is how we will go about it. We need to start with a page break,

---

2. Of course you can use the frametricks package to get around this limitation—split the current frame and start fiddling around with the positions of the new frames that frametricks created for you.

because SILE will not appreciate you changing the page layout after it's started to determine how to put text onto that page.[2] How do we get to the start of a new page? Remember that the \eject (another word for \break in vertical mode) only adds a penalty to the end of the output queue; page breaking is triggered when we leave horizontal mode, and the way to do that is \par. So we start with \eject\par and then we will begin a \pagetemplate. Within \pagetemplate we need to tell SILE which frame to being typesetting onto.

```
\eject\par
\begin[first-content-frame=leftCol]{pagetemplate}
```

Now we will declare our columns. But we're actually going to start by declaring the gutter first, because that's something that we know and can define; we're going to stipulate that the gutter width will be 3% of the page width:

```
\frame[id=gutter,width=3%]
```

Declarations of frame dimensions are like ordinary SILE *<dimension>s, except with three additional features:*

• You can refer to properties of other frames using the top(), bottom(), left(), right(), height() *and* width() *functions. These functions take a frame ID.* SILE *magically pre-defines the frame* page *to allow you to access the dimensions of the whole page.*

• You can use arithmetic functions: plus, minus, divide, multiply and brackets have their ordinary arithmetic meaning. To declare that frame b should be half the height of frame a plus 5 millimeters, you can say height=5mm + (height(b) / 2). *However as we will see later it is usually better to structure*

> *your declarations to let SILE make those kind of computations for you.*
> *• Since book design is often specified in terms of proportion of a page, you can use the shortcut* width=5% *instead of* width=0.05 * width(page) *and* height=50% *instead of* height=0.5 * height(page). *SILE knows whether you're dealing with vertical or horizontal percentages.*

Next we declare the left and right column frames. The book class gives us some frames already, one of which, r, is a standard right-hand page. We will use the boundaries of this frame to declare our columns: the left margin of the left column is the left margin of the typeblock; the right margin of the right column is the right margin of the typeblock. But we also want a few other parameters to ensure that:

• the gutter is placed between our two columns

• the two columns have the same width (We don't know what that width is, but SILE will work it out for us.)

• after the left column is full, typesetting should move to the right column.

```
\frame[id=leftCol, left=left(r), right=left(gutter),
       top=top(r), bottom=bottom(r),
       next=rightCol]
\frame[id=rightCol, left=right(gutter), right=right(r),
       top=top(r), bottom=bottom(r),
       width=width(leftCol)]
```

And now finally we can end our pagetemplate.

```
\end{pagetemplate}
```

Let's do it.

leftCol

rightCol

So there we have it: a two-column page layout.

In the next chapter we'll use the knowledge of how to declare frames to help us to create our own document class files. In the meantime, here is some dummy text to demonstrate the fact that text does indeed flow between the two columns naturally:

lorem ipsum dolor sit amet consetetur sadipscing elitr sed diam nonumy eirmod tempor invidunt ut labore et dolore magna aliquyam erat sed diam voluptua at vero eos et accusam et justo duo dolores et ea rebum stet clita kasd gubergren no sea takimata sanctus est lorem ipsum dolor sit amet lorem ipsum dolor sit amet consetetur sadipscing elitr sed diam nonumy eirmod tempor invidunt ut labore et dolore magna aliquyam erat sed diam voluptua at vero eos et accusam et justo duo dolores et ea rebum stet clita kasd gubergren no sea takimata sanctus est lorem ipsum dolor sit amet lorem ipsum dolor sit amet consetetur sadipscing elitr sed diam nonumy eirmod tempor invidunt ut labore et dolore magna aliquyam erat sed diam voluptua at vero eos et accusam et justo duo dolores et ea rebum stet clita kasd gubergren no sea takimata sanctus est lorem ipsum dolor sit amet

duis autem vel eum iriure dolor

in hendrerit in vulputate velit esse molestie consequat vel illum dolore eu feugiat nulla facilisis at vero eros et accumsan et iusto odio dignissim qui blandit praesent luptatum zzril delenit augue duis dolore te feugait nulla facilisi lorem ipsum dolor sit amet consectetuer

The Nitty Gritty

Chapter 9
Designing Basic Class Files

Now we know how to define a frame layout for a single page, let's try to define one for an entire document.

Document classes are Lua files, and live somewhere in the classes/ subdirectory of either your current directory or your SILE path (typically /usr/local/share/sile). We're going to create a simple class file which merely changes the size of the margins and the typeblock. We'll call it bringhurst.lua, because it replicates the layout of the Hartley & Marks edition of Robert Bringhurst's *The Elements of Typographical Style*.

We are designing a book-like class, and so we will inherit from SILE's standard book class, classes/book.lua.

Let's briefly have a look at book.lua to see how it works; after the initial class definition, we see the following frame declarations: (wrapped for legibility)

```
book:declareFrame("r",      {left = "8.3%",
                             right = "86%",
                             top = "11.6%",
                             bottom = "top(footnotes)"
                            });
book:declareFrame("folio",{left = "left(r)",
                             right = "right(r)",
                             top = "bottom(footnotes)+3%",
                             bottom = "bottom(footnotes)+5%"
                            });
book:declareFrame("rRH",    {left = "left(r)",
                             right = "right(r)",
                             top = "top(r) - 8%",
                             bottom = "top(r)-3%"
                            });
```

```
book:declareFrame("footnotes", { left="left(r)",
                              right = "right(r)",
                              height = "0",
                              bottom="83.3%"
                        });
```

So there are four frames directly declared; the first is the right-hand master frame, which by SILE convention is called r. Directly abutting the r frame at the bottom is the footnotes frame. The top of the typeblock and the bottom of the footnote frame have fixed positions, but the boundary between typeblock and footnote is variable. Initially the height of the footnotes is zero (and so the typeblock takes up the full height of the page) but as footnotes are inserted into the footnote frame, its height will be adjusted; its bottom is fixed and therefore its top will be adjusted, and the bottom of the main typeblock frame will also be correspondingly adjusted.

The folio frame (the page number) lives below the footnotes, and the running headers live above the r frame.

Next, we use the twoside package to mirror our right-page frames into left-page frames:

```
book:loadPackage("twoside",
oddPageFrameID = "r", evenPageFrameID = "l" );
book:declareMirroredFrame("l","r")
book:declareMirroredFrame("lRH","rRH")
```

Since we will be inheriting from the book class, we will have all these definitions already available to us. All we need to do is set up our new class, and then define what is different about it. Here is how we set up the inheritance:

```
local book = SILE.require("classes/book")
local bringhurst = book  id = "bringhurst"
...
return bringhurst
```

Now we need to define our frames.

The LaTeX memoir class' *A Few Notes On Book Design* tells us that Bringhurst's book has a spine margin one thirteenth of the page width; a top margin eight-fifths of the spine margin; a front margin and bottom margin both sixteen-fifths of the spine margin. We can define this in SILE terms like so:

```
bringhurst:declareFrame("r", {
  left = "width(page)/13",
  top = "left(r) * 8 / 5",
  right = "100% - 2*top(r)",
  bottom = "top(footnotes)"
})
bringhurst:declareFrame("footnotes", {
  left="left(r)",
  right = "right(r)",
  height = "0",
  bottom = "100% - 2*top(r)"
})
```

We are nearly finished!

If we try this class as-is, we'll actually find that the running headers are too high, because the typeblock is higher on the page than the standard book class, and the running heads are defined relative to them.

So, we need to also declare the running header frame to bring them down a bit lower:

```
bringhurst:declareFrame("rRH", {
  left = "left(r)",
  right = "right(r)",
  top = "top(r) - 4%",
  bottom = "top(r)-2%"
});
```

If all we want to do in our new class is to create a different page shape, this is all we need.

9.1 Defining Commands

However, it's usually the case that a class will want to do more than just change the page shape; a class will typically want to do some other things as well: define additional commands, alter the output routine, store and investigate bits of state information, and so on. We'll look briefly at some of the principles involved in those things here, and in the next chapters will run through some worked examples.

To define your own command at the Lua level, you use the SILE.registerCommand function. It takes three parameters: a command name, a function to implement the command, and some help text. The signature of a function representing a SILE command is fixed: you need to take two parameters, options and content (of course you can name your parameters whatever you like, but these are the most common names). Both of these parameters are Lua tables. The options parameter contains the command's parameters or XML attributes as a key-value table, and the content is an abstract syntax tree reflecting the input being currently processed.

So in the case of \mycommand[size=12pt]{Hello \break world}, the first parameter will contain the table {size = "12pt"} and the second parameter will contain the table

```
"Hello ",

  attr = ,
  id = "command",
  pos = 8,
  tag = "break"
,
" world"
```

Most commands will find themselves doing something with the `options` and/or calling `SILE.process(content)` to recursively process the argument. Here's a very simple example; an XML `<link>` tag may take an XLink `xl:href` attribute[1] We want to render `<link xl:href="http://...">Hello</link>` as Hello (`http://...`). So, first we need to render the content, and then we need to do something with the attribute:

```
SILE.registerCommand("link", function(options, content)
  SILE.process(content)
  if (options["xl:href"]) then
    SILE.typesetter:typeset(" (")
    SILE.call("code", , options["xl:href"])
    SILE.typesetter:typeset(")")
  end
end)
```

We use the usual `SILE.typesetter:typeset` and `SILE.call` functions to output text and call other commands.

If you do need to do something with a dimension, you can use `SILE.toPoints` *to parse a basic length and* `SILE.parseComplexFrameDimension` *to parse*

1. Yes, I know the document author might choose a different XML namespace to refer to XLink. Let's keep things simple.

a frame dimension, and turn them into points.

9.2 Output Routines

As well as defining frames and packages, different classes also alter the way that SILE performs its output–what it should do at the start or end of a page, for instance, which controls things like swapping between different master frames, displaying page numbers, and so on.

The key methods for defining the *output routine* are:

• newPar and endPar are called at the start and end of each paragraph.

• newPage and endPage are called at the start and each of each page.

• init and finish are called at the start and end of the document.

Once again this is done in an object-oriented way, with derived classes overriding their superclass' methods where necessary.

When you are loading packages which affect the output routine, the composition of such packages into a class is not completely automatic[2]; in other words, loading the package will not necessarily by itself change the output routines. You need to explicitly plug the various features provided by those packages into the output routine yourself.

So, for instance, the footnote or insertions packages provide a outputInsertions method which needs to be called at the end of each page. If you want to build a document class that inherits from plain but also has footnote functionality, you will want your endPage method to look like this:

```
myClass.endPage = function(self)
  myClass:outputInsertions()
  plain.endPage(self)
```

---

2. Because the order of events is sometimes significant.

```
end
```

Let's demonstrate roughly how the tableofcontents package works. We'll be using the infonodes package to collect the information about which pages contain table of content items.

First, we set up our infonodes by creating a command that can be called by sectioning commands. In other words, \chapter, \section, etc. should call \tocentry to store the page reference for this section.

```
SILE.registerCommand("tocentry", function (options, content)
  SILE.call("info", {
    category = "toc",
    value = {
      label = content, level = (options.level or 1)
    }
  })
end)
```

Infonodes work on a per-page basis, so if we want to save them throughout the whole document, at the end of each page we need to move them from the per-page table to our own table. We also need to make sure we store their page numbers!

> *SILE provides the* SILE.scratch *variable for you to store global information in; you should use a portion of this table namespaced to your class or package.*

So, here is a routine we can call at the end of each page to move the TOC nodes.

```
SILE.scratch.tableofcontents =
% Gather the tocentries into a big document-wide TOC
```

```
local moveNodes = function(self)
  local n = SILE.scratch.info.thispage.toc
  for i=1,#n do
    n[i].pageno = SILE.formatCounter(SILE.scratch.counters.folio)
    table.insert(SILE.scratch.tableofcontents, n[i])
  end
end
```

We're going to take the LaTeX approach of storing these items out as a separate file, then loading them back in again when typesetting the TOC. So at the end of the document, we serialize the SILE.scratch. tableofcontents table to disk. Here is a function to be called by the finish output routine.

```
local writeToc = function (self)
  local t = std.string.pickle(SILE.scratch.tableofcontents)
  saveFile(t, SILE.masterFileName .. '.toc')
end
```

And then the \tableofcontents command reads that file if it is present, and typesets the TOC nodes appropriately:

```
SILE.registerCommand("tableofcontents", function (options, content)
  local toc = loadFile(SILE.masterFileName .. '.toc')
  if not toc then
    SILE.call("tableofcontents:notocmessage")
    return
  end
  SILE.call("tableofcontents:header")
  for i = 1,#toc do
    local item = toc[i]
    SILE.call("tableofcontents:item",
```

```
level = item.level, pageno= item.pageno, item.label)
  end
end)
```

And the job is done. Well, nearly. The `tableofcontents` package now contains a couple of functions–moveNodes and writeToc–that need to be called at various points in the output routine of a class which uses this package. How do we do that?

9.3 Exports

Packages which are primarily used for providing functionality to other classes and packages need a way of supplying these composible bits of functionality to the code which is going to use them. This is called the *export mechanism*.

As well as defining commands, each package may also return a Lua table consisting of two entries, `init` and `exports`.

`init` allows you to perform some initialization actions, optionally based on arguments supplied by the loading class. When the package is loaded with `class:loadPackage(package, args)`, the initializer is called with two arguments, `class` and `args`. For instance, the `twoside` package receives information about the IDs of the main right and left master frames so that it can set up the code to switch masters on page change. In our case, we will want to ensure that the `infonode` package is loaded into our caller:

```
return {
  init = function (caller)
    caller:loadPackage("infonode")
  end,
```

The other entry to be returned from the package is exports, which contains names and functions to be mixed into the caller's namespace. In other words, after:

```
  exports = writeToc = writeToc, moveTocNodes = moveNodes
}
```

---

any class which loads tableofcontents can call self:writeToc() and self:moveTocNodes() (note that we renamed this function when exporting it). It is the class's responsibility for calling these methods at the appropriate point into the output routine.

Chapter 10
Advanced Class Files: SILE As An XML Processor

Now we are ready to look at a worked example of writing a class to turn an arbitrary XML format into a PDF file. We'll be looking at the DocBook processor that ships with SILE. DocBook is an XML format for structured technical documentation. DocBook itself doesn't encode any presentation information about how its various tags should be rendered on a page, and so we shall have to make all the presentation decisions for ourself.

The first thing you should know is that it makes your life significantly easier if you consider writing the class file in *two* files; the first being a SILE file in TeX format, and the second as Lua code. This allows you to dispose of all the easy jobs in a convenient format, and then deal with the hard jobs in Lua. When you use the -I *classname* command line option to SILE, SILE first looks for *classname*.sil and uses that as a wrapper around your file to be processed. If that then begins

```
\begin[papersize=a4,class=classname]{document}
```

then SILE will also load up classes/*classname*.lua as normal.

Now we can start defining SILE commands to render XML elements. Most of these are fairly straightforward so we will not dwell on them too much. For instance, DocBook has a tags like <code>, <filename>, <guimenu> which should all be rendered in a monospaced typewriter font. To make it easier to customize the class, we abstract out the font change into a single command:

```
\define[command=docbook-
```

```
ttfont]{\font[family=Inconsolata,size=2ex]{\process}}
```

Now we can define our <code> (etc.) tags:

```
\define[command=code]{\docbook-ttfont{\process}}
\define[command=filename]{\docbook-ttfont{\process}}
\define[command=guimenu]{\docbook-ttfont{\process}}
\define[command=guilabel]{\docbook-ttfont{\process}}
\define[command=guibutton]{\docbook-ttfont{\process}}
\define[command=computeroutput]{\docbook-ttfont{\process}}
```

If an end user wants things to look different, they can redefine the docbook-ttfont command and get a different font.

10.1 Handling Titles

So much for simple tags. Things get interesting when there is a mismatch between the simple format of SILE macros and the complexity of Doc-Book markup.

We have already seen an example of the <link> tag where we also need to process XML attributes, so we will not repeat that here. Let's look at another area of complexity: the apparently-simple <title> tag. The reason this is complex is that it occurs in different contexts, sometimes more than once within a context; it should often be rendered differently in different contexts. So for instance <article><title>... will look different to <section><title>.... Inside an <example> tag, the title will be preferenced by an example number; inside a <bibliomixed> bibliography entry the title should not be set off as a new block but should be part of the running text, and so on.

What we will do to deal with this situation is provide a very simple definition of <title>, but when processing the containing elements of <title> (such as <article>, <example>), we will process the title ourselves.

For instance, let's look at <example>, which has the added complexity of needed to keep track of an article number.

```
SILE.registerCommand("example", function(options,content)
  SILE.call("increment-counter", id="Example")
  SILE.call("bigskip")
  SILE.call("docbook-line")
  SILE.call("docbook-titling", , function()
    SILE.typesetter:typeset("Example".."
".. SILE.formatCounter(SILE.scratch.counters.Example]))
```

\docbook-line is a command that we've defined in the docbook.sil macros file to draw a line across the width of the page to set off examples and so on. \docbook-titling is a command similarly defined in docbook.sil which sets the default font for titling and headers; once again, if people want to customize the look of the output we make it easier for them by giving them simple, compartmentalized commands to override.

So far so good, but how do we extract the <title> tag from the content abstract syntax tree? SILE does not provide XPath or CSS-style selectors to locate content form within the DOM tree;[1] instead there is a simple one-level function called SILE.findInTree which looks for a particular tag or command name within the immediate children of the current tree:

```
local t = SILE.findInTree(content, "title")
if t then
  SILE.typesetter:typeset(": ")
  SILE.process(t)
```

We've output Example 123 so far, and now we need to say : *Title*. But we also need to ensure that the <title> tag doesn't get processed again when we process the content of the example:

---

1. Patches, as they say, are welcome.

```
docbook.wipe(t)
```

`docbook.wipe` is a little helper function which nullifies all the content of a Lua table:

```
function docbook.wipe(tbl)
  while((#tbl) > 0) do tbl[#tbl] = nil end
end
```

Let's finish off the `<example>` example by skipping a big between the title and the content, processing the content and drawing a final line across the page:

```
    end
  end)
  SILE.call("smallskip")
  SILE.process(content)
  SILE.call("docbook-line")
  SILE.call("bigskip")
```

Now it happens that the `<example>`, `<table>` and `<figure>` tags are pretty equivalent: they produce numbered titles and then go on to process their content. So in reality we actually define an abstract `countedThing` method and define these commands in terms of that.

10.2 Sectioning

DocBook sectioning is a little different to the SILE book class. `<section>` tags can be nested; to start a subsection, you place another `<section>` tag inside the current `<section>`. So in order to know what level we are currently on, we need a stack; we also need to keep track of what section number we are on at *each* level. For instance:

```
<section><title>A</title>  :  1. A
```

```
<section><title>B</title>: 1.1  B
</section>
<section><title>C</title>: 1.2  C
  <section><title>D</title>: 1.2.1  D
  </section>
</section>
<section><title>E</title>: 1.3  E
</section>
<section><title>F</title>: 2.  F
```

So, we will keep two variables: the current level, and the counters for all of the levels so far. Each time we enter a section, we increase the current level counter:

```
SILE.registerCommand("section", function (options, content)
  SILE.scratch.docbook.seclevel = SILE.scratch.docbook.seclevel + 1
```

We also increment the count at the current level, while at the same time wiping out any counts we have for levels above the current level (if we didn't do that, then E in our example above would be marked 1.3.1):

```
  SILE.scratch.docbook.seccount[SILE.scratch.docbook.seclevel] =
    (SILE.scratch.docbook.seccount[SILE.scratch.docbook.seclevel]
or 0) + 1
  while
#(SILE.scratch.docbook.seccount) > SILE.scratch.docbook.seclevel do
SILE.scratch.docbook.seccount[#(SILE.scratch.docbook.seccount)] = nil
  end
```

Now we find the title, and prefix it by the concatenation of all the seccounts:

```
  local title = SILE.findInTree(content, "title")
  local number = table.concat(SILE.scratch.docbook.seccount, '.')
  if title then
    SILE.call("docbook-
section-"..SILE.scratch.docbook.seclevel.."-title",{},function()
```

```
    SILE.typesetter:typeset(number.." ")
    SILE.process(title)
  end)
  docbook.wipe(title)
end
```

Finally we can process the content of the tag, and decrease the level count as we leave the </section> tag:

```
SILE.process(content)
SILE.scratch.docbook.seclevel = SILE.scratch.docbook.seclevel - 1
end)
```

10.3 Other Features

SILE's DocBook implementation is a work in progress, and there is more that can be done. For instance, there is a basic implementation of lists, which equally need to be able to handle nesting; we implement another stack to take care of the type of list and list counter at each level of nesting.

How would you handle a tag like <xref> which renders a cross-reference to another part of the document? For instance, <xref linkend="ch02"/> should generate something like Chapter 2, "The Second Chapter". This is another problem which can be handled using the infonode package to collect and store cross-reference information about chapter numbers and titles.

Chapter 11
Further Tricks

We'll conclude our tour of SILE by looking at some tricky situations which require further programming.

11.1 Parallel Text

The file `examples/parallel.sil` contains a rendering of chapter 1 of Matthew's Gospel in English and Greek. It uses the `diglot` class to align the two texts side-by-side. `diglot` provides the `\left` and `\right` commands to start entering text on the left column or the right column respectively, and the `\sync` command to ensure that the two columns are in sync with each other. It's an instructive example of what can be done in a SILE class, so we will take it apart and see how it works.

The key thing to note is that the SILE typesetter is an object. (in the object-oriented programming sense) Normally, it's a singleton object–i.e. one typesetter is used for typesetting everything in a document. But there's no reason why we can't have more than one. In fact, for typesetting parallel texts, the simplest way to do things is to have two typesetters, one for each column, and have them communicate with each other at various points in the operation.

Let's begin `diglot.lua` as usual by setting up the class and declaring our frames:

```
local plain = SILE.require("classes/plain");
local diglot = std.tree.clone(plain);
SILE.require("packages/counters");
SILE.scratch.counters.folio = { value = 1, display = "arabic" };
SILE.scratch.diglot = {}
diglot:declareFrame("a",     {left = "8.3%", right = "48%",
```

```
          top = "11.6%", bottom = "80%" });
diglot:declareFrame("b",    {left = "52%",  right = "100% - left(a)",
          top = "top(a)", bottom = "bottom(a)" });
diglot:declareFrame("folio",{left = "left(a)", right = "right(b)",
          top = "bottom(a)+3%",bottom = "bottom(a)+8%" });
```

Now we create two new typesetters, one for each column, and we tell each one how to find the other:

```
diglot.leftTypesetter = SILE.defaultTypesetter {}
diglot.rightTypesetter = SILE.defaultTypesetter {}
diglot.rightTypesetter.other = diglot.leftTypesetter
diglot.leftTypesetter.other = diglot.rightTypesetter
```

Each column needs its own font, so we provide commands to store this information. The \leftfont and \rightfont macros simply store their options to be passed to the \font command every time \left and \right are called. (Because the fonts are controlled by global settings rather than being typesetter-specific.)

```
SILE.registerCommand("leftfont", function(options, content)
  SILE.scratch.diglot.leftfont = options
end, "Set the font for the left side")

SILE.registerCommand("rightfont", function(options, content)
  SILE.scratch.diglot.rightfont = options
end, "Set the font for the right side")
```

Next come the commands for sending text to the appropriate type-setter. The current typesetter object used by the system is stored in the variable SILE.typesetter; many commands and packages call methods on this variable, so we need to ensure that this is set to the typesetter object that we want to use. We also want to turn off paragraph detection, as we will be handling the paragraphing manually using the \sync command:

73

```
SILE.registerCommand("left", function(options, content)
  SILE.settings.set("typesetter.parseppattern", -1)
  SILE.typesetter = diglot.leftTypesetter;
  SILE.Commands["font"](SILE.scratch.diglot.leftfont, )
end, "Begin entering text on the left side")

SILE.registerCommand("right", function(options, content)
  SILE.settings.set("typesetter.parseppattern", -1)
  SILE.typesetter = diglot.rightTypesetter;
  SILE.Commands["font"](SILE.scratch.diglot.rightfont, )
end, "Begin entering text on the right side")
```

The meat of the diglot package comes in the sync command, which ensures that the two typesetters are aligned. Every time we call sync, we want to ensure that they are both at the same position on the page. In other words, if the left typesetter has gone further down the page than the right one, we need to insert some blank space onto the right type-setter's output queue to get them back in sync, and vice versa.

SILE's page builder has a method called SILE.pagebuilder.collateVboxes which bundles a bunch of vertical boxes into one; we can use this to bundle up each typesetter's output queue and measure the height of the combined vbox. (Of course it's possible to sum the heights of each box on the output queue by hand, but this achieves the same goal a bit more cleanly.)

```
SILE.registerCommand("sync", function()
  local lVbox =
SILE.pagebuilder.collateVboxes(diglot.leftTypesetter.state.outputQueue)
  local rVbox =
SILE.pagebuilder.collateVboxes(diglot.rightTypesetter.state.outputQueue)
  if (rVbox.height > lVbox.height) then
    diglot.leftTypesetter:pushVglue(
height = rVbox.height - lVbox.height )
  elseif (rVbox.height < lVbox.height) then
    diglot.rightTypesetter:pushVglue(
height = lVbox.height - rVbox.height )
  end
```

Next we end each paragraph (we do this after adding the glue so that parskips do not get in the way), and go back to handling paragraphing as normal:

```
diglot.rightTypesetter:leaveHmode();
diglot.leftTypesetter:leaveHmode();
SILE.settings.set("typesetter.parseppattern", "\n\n+")
end)
```

Now everything is ready apart from the output routine. In the output routine we need to ensure, at the start of each document and the start of each page, that each typesetter is linked to the appropriate frame:

```
diglot.init = function(self)
  diglot.leftTypesetter:init(SILE.getFrame("a"))
  diglot.rightTypesetter:init(SILE.getFrame("b"))
  return SILE.baseClass.init(self)
end
```

(SILE.getFrame retrieves a frame that we have declared.)

The default newPage routine will do this for one typesetter every time we open a new page, but it doesn't know that we have another typesetter object to set up as well; so we need to to make sure that, no matter which typesetter causes an new-page event, the other typesetter also gets correctly initialised:

```
diglot.newPage = function(self)
  plain.newPage(self)
  if SILE.typesetter == diglot.leftTypesetter then
    SILE.typesetter.other:initFrame(SILE.getFrame("b"))
    return SILE.getFrame("a")
  else
    SILE.typesetter.other:initFrame(SILE.getFrame("a"))
    return SILE.getFrame("b")
```

```
  end
end
```

And finally, when one typesetter causes an end-of-page event, we need to ensure that the other typesetter is given the opportunity to output its queue to the page as well:

```
diglot.endPage = function(self)
  SILE.typesetter.other:leaveHmode(1)
  plain.endPage(self)
end
```

Similarly for the end of the document, but in this case we will use the emergency chuck method; whereas leaveHmode means "call the page builder and see there's enough material to build a page", chuck means "you must get rid of everything on your queue now." We add some infinitely tall glue to the other typesetter's queue to help the process along:

```
diglot.finish = function(self)
  table.insert(SILE.typesetter.other.state.outputQueue,
SILE.nodefactory.vfillGlue)
  SILE.typesetter.other:chuck()
  plain.finish(self)
end
```

And there you have it; a class which produces balanced parallel texts using two typesetters at once.

11.2 Sidenotes

One SILE project needed two different kinds of sidenotes, margin notes and gutter notes.

Chapter 9

The Transfiguration

9:1 Matt.
16:28; Mark
13:26; Luke
9:27

[1]And Jesus was saying[xxx] to them," **Truly** I say to you, ⌈there are some of those who are standing here who will **not** taste death until they see the kingdom of God after it has come[*] with power⌉."

Sidenotes can be seen as a simplified form of parallel text. With a true parallel, neither the left or the right typesetter is "in charge"–either can fill up the page and then inform the other typesetter that they need to catch up. In the case of sidenotes, there's a well-defined main flow of text, with annotations having to work around the pagination of the type-block.

There are a variety of ways that we could implement these side-notes; as it happened, I chose a different strategy for the margin notes and the gutter notes. Cross-references in the gutter could appear fairly frequently, and so needed to "stack up" down the page–they need to be *at least* on a level with the verse that they relate to, but could end up further down the page if there are a few cross-references close to each other. Markings in the margin, on the other hand, were guaranteed not to overlap.

We'll look at the margin marking first. We'll implement this as a special zero-width hbox (what TeX would call a \special) which, although it lives in the output stream of the main typeblock, actually outputs itself by marking the margin at the current vertical position in the typeblock. In the example above, there will be a special hbox just before the word "there" in the first line.

First we need to find the appropriate margin frame and, find its left boundary:

```
discovery.typesetProphecy = function(symbol)
  local margin = discovery:oddPage() and
SILE.getFrame("rMargin") or SILE.getFrame("lMargin")
```

```
local target = margin:left()
```

Next, we call another command to produce the symbol itself; this allows the book designer to change the symbols at the SILE level rather than having to mess about with the Lua file. We use the \hbox command to wrap the output of the command into a hbox. \hbox returns its output, but also puts the box into the typesetter's output node queue; we don't want it to appear in the main typeblock, so we remove the node again, leaving our private copy in the hbox variable.

```
local hbox = SILE.call("hbox",{}, function()
  SILE.call("prophecy-"..symbol.."-mark")
end)
table.remove(SILE.typesetter.state.nodes)
```

What we *do* want in the output queue is our special hbox node which will put the marking into the margin. This special hbox has no impact on the current line–it has no width, height, or depth–and it contains a copy of the symbol that we stored in the hbox variable.

```
SILE.typesetter:pushHbox({
  width= 0,
  height = 0,
  depth= 0,
  value= hbox,
```

Finally we need to write the routine which outputs this hbox. Box output routines receive three parameters: the box itself, the current typesetter (which knows the frame it is typesetting into, and the frame knows whereabouts it has got to), and a variable representing the stretchability or shrinkability of the line. (We don't need that for this example.)

What our output routine should do is: save a copy of our horizontal position, so that we can restore it later as we carry on outputting other boxes; jump across to the left edge of the margin, which we computed previously; tell the symbol that we're carrying with us to output *itself*; and then jump back to where we were:

```
outputYourself= function (self, typesetter, line)
  local saveX = typesetter.frame.state.cursorX;
  typesetter.frame.state.cursorX = target
  self.value:outputYourself(typesetter,line)
  typesetter.frame.state.cursorX = saveX
end
})
```

This was a quick-and-dirty version of sidenotes (in twenty lines of code!) which works reasonably well for individual symbols which are guaranteed not to overlap. For the gutter notes, which are closer to true sidenotes, we need to do something a bit more intelligent. We'll take a similar approach to when we made the parallel texts, by employing a separate typesetter object.

As before we'll create the object, and ensure that at the start of the document and at the start of each page it is populated correctly with the appropriate frame:

```
discovery.innerTypesetter = SILE.defaultTypesetter {}

discovery.init = function()
  local gutter = discovery:oddPage() and
                 SILE.getFrame("rGutter") or SILE.getFrame("lGutter")
  discovery.innerTypesetter:init(gutter)
  ...
  return SILE.baseClass:init()
end

discovery.newPage = function ()
  ...
  discovery.innerTypesetter:leaveHmode(1)
  local gutter = discovery:oddPage() and
                 SILE.getFrame("rGutter") or SILE.getFrame("lGutter")
  discovery.innerTypesetter:init(gutter)
  ...
```

```
  return SILE.baseClass.newPage(discovery);
end
```

Now for the function which actually handles a cross-reference. As with the parallels example, we start by totting up the height of the material processed on the current page by both the main typesetter and the cross-reference typesetter.

```
discovery.typesetCrossReference = function(xref)
  discovery.innerTypesetter:leaveHmode(1)
  local innerVbox =
SILE.pagebuilder.collateVboxes(discovery.innerTypesetter.state.outputQueue)
  local mainVbox
= SILE.pagebuilder.collateVboxes(SILE.typesetter.state.outputQueue)
```

This deals with the material which has already been put into the output queue: in other words, completed paragraphs. The problem here is that we do not want to end a paragraph between two verses; if we are mid-paragraph while typesetting a cross-reference, we need to work out what the height of the material *would have been* if we were to put it onto the output queue at this point. So, we take the SILE.typesetter object on a little excursion.

First we take a copy of the current node queue, and then we call the typesetter's pushState method. This initializes the typesetter anew, while saving its existing state for later. Since we have a new typesetter, its node queue is empty, and so we feed it the nodes that represent our paragraph so far. Then we tell the typesetter to leave horizontal mode, which will cause it to go away and calculate line breaks, leading, paragraph height and so on. We box up its output queue, and then return to where we were before. Now we have a box which represents what would happen if we set the current paragraph up to the point that our cross-reference is inserted; the height of this box is the distance we need to add to mainVbox to get the vertical position of the cross-reference mark.

```
local unprocessedNodes = std.tree.clone(SILE.typesetter.state.nodes)
  SILE.typesetter:pushState()
  SILE.typesetter.state.nodes = unprocessedNodes
  SILE.typesetter:leaveHmode(1)
  local subsidiary
= SILE.pagebuilder.collateVboxes(SILE.typesetter.state.outputQueue)
  SILE.typesetter:popState()
  mainVbox.height = mainVbox.height + subsidiary.height
```

The 1 argument to leaveHmode *means "you may not create a new page here."*

In most cases, the cross-reference typesetter hasn't got as far down the page as the body text typesetter, so we tell the cross-reference typesetter to shift itself down the page by the difference. Unlike the parallel example, where either typesetter could tell the other to open up additional vertical space, in this case it's OK if the cross-reference appears a bit lower than the verse it refers to.

```
if (innerVbox.height < mainVbox.height) then
   discovery.innerTypesetter:pushVglue(
height = mainVbox.height - innerVbox.height )
   end
```

At this point the two typesetters are now either aligned, or the cross-reference typesetter has gone further down the page than the verse it refers to. Now we can output the cross-reference itself.

```
SILE.settings.temporarily(function()
   SILE.settings.set("document.baselineskip",
SILE.nodefactory.newVglue("7pt"))
   SILE.Commands["font"](size
= "6pt", family="Helvetica", weight="800", )
discovery.innerTypesetter:typeset(SILE.scratch.chapter..":"..SILE.scratch.v
")
   SILE.Commands["font"](size
= "6pt", family="Helvetica", weight="200", )
```

```
    discovery.innerTypesetter:typeset(xref)
    discovery.innerTypesetter:leaveHmode()
    discovery.innerTypesetter:pushVglue(
height = SILE.length.new(length = 4) )
  end)
end
```

> We haven't used SILE.call *here because it performs all its operations on the default typesetter. If we wanted to make things cleaner, we could swap typesetters by assigning* discovery.innerTypesetter *to* SILE.typesetter *and then calling ordinary commands, rather than doing the settings and glue insertion "by hand."*

In the future it may make sense for there to be a standard sidenotes package in SILE, but it has been instructive to see a couple of 'non-standard' examples to understand how the internals of SILE can be leveraged to create such a package. Your homework is to create one!

11.3 SILE As A Library

So far we've been assuming that you would want to run SILE as a processor for an existing document. But what if you have a program which produces or munges data, and you would like to produce PDFs from within your application? In that case, it may be easier and provide more flexibility to use SILE as a library.

In the examples/ directory of the SILE distribution, you will find an example of a Lua script which produces a PDF from SILE. It's actually fairly simple to use SILE from within Lua; the difficult part is setting things up. Here's how to do it.

```
require("core/sile")
```

```
SILE.outputFilename = "byhand.pdf"
local plain = require("classes/plain")
plain.options.papersize("a4")
SILE.documentState.documentClass = plain;
local ff = plain:init()
SILE.typesetter:init(ff)
```

Loading the SILE core library also loads up all the other parts of SILE. We need to set the output file name and load the class that we want to use to typeset the document with. As with an ordinary SILE document, the papersize option is mandatory, so we call the options.papersize method of our document class to set the paper size. We then need to tell SILE what class we are actually using, call init on the class to get the first frame for typesetting, and then initialize the typesetter with this frame. This is all that SILE does to get itself ready to typeset.

After this, all the usual API calls will work: SILE.call, SILE.typesetter: and so on.

```
SILE.typesetter:typeset(data)
```

The only thing to be careful is the need to call the finish method on your document class at the end of processing to finish off the final page:

```
plain:finish()
```

11.4 Debugging

When you are experimenting with SILE and its API, you may find it necessary to get further information about what SILE is up to. SILE has a variety of debugging switches that can be turned on by the command line or by Lua code.

Running SILE with the --debug *facility* switch will turn on debugging for a particular area of SILE's operation:

• typesetter provides general debugging for the typesetter: turning characters into boxes, boxes into lines, lines into paragraphs, and paragraphs into pages.

• pagebuilder helps to debug problems when determining page breaks.

• break provides (copious) information about the line breaking algorithm.

• Any package may define their own debugging facility; currently only insertions does this.

Multiple facilities can be turned on by separating them with commas: --debug typesetter,break will turn on debugging information for the typesetter and line breaker.

From Lua, you can add entries to the SILE.debugFlags table to turn on debugging for a given facility. This can be useful for temporarily debugging a particular operation:

```
SILE.debugFlags.typesetter = 1
SILE.typesetter:leaveHmode()
SILE.debugFlags.typesetter = nil
```

From a package's point of view, you can write debugging information by calling the SU.debug function (SU stands for SILE Utilities, and contains a variety of auxiliary functions used throughout SILE):

```
SU.debug("mypackage", "Doing a thing")
```

Sometimes it's useful for you to try out Lua code within the SILE environment; SILE contains a REPL (read-evaluate-print loop) for you to enter Lua code and print the results back to you. If you call SILE with no input file name, it enters the REPL:

```
This is SILE 0.9.0
> l = SILE.length.parse("22mm")
> l.length
62.3622054
```

At any point during the evaluation of Lua commands, you can call SILE.repl() to enter the REPL and poke around; hitting Ctrl-D will end the REPL and return to processing the document.

11.5 Conclusion

We've seen not just the basic functionality of SILE but also given you some examples of how to extend it in new directions; how to use the SILE API to solve difficult problems in typesetting. Go forth and create your own SILE packages!

Index of Commands

Index of Settings

Index of Settings